Praying Deeper through the Psalms for Children

Author – Lynda Freeman

Collaborators & Illustrators - Josiah, Caleb & Shane Freeman

Look What People are Saying . . .

I love this book. One of the best elements is how it is set up on different developmental levels. No matter the age of your child, they will find comfort in the Word of God, because they will be better able to understand the message. "Praying Deeper Through the Psalms for Children" is one of the best resources a grandparent, parent or Bible study teacher will give to a child.

Linda Ranson Jacobs
Mom, Grandma, Author, "The Single Parent Confident & Successful"
Founder/Creator of DC4K -Divorce Care for Kids, Church Initiative
Ministry Ambassador

"Praying Deeper Through the Psalms for Children" is a wonderful, insightful, and practical devotional book for loving adults to guide their children or grandchildren through. I love that the the author's grandchildren contributed to the art in the book, which will certainly engage young readers. I look forward to guiding my son through this helpful resource.

Pastor Karl Bastian - Dad, founder of Kidology.org

I love this joint project created by Lynda and her grandsons! "Praying Through the Psalms for Children" will help grandparents and parents be intentional in prayer and Bible reading with their grandchildren. It is easy to see how this book will enable grandparents and parents to pray more effectively for and with the children they love.

As a children's ministry professional, I'm happy to see resources created for grandparents/parents to help encourage a strong faith in the next generation. Grandparents are the second greatest influence in the lives of their grandchildren; what they do matters. This book is a helpful tool for special time together.

Jane Larson - Mom, Children's Ministry Speaker,
Legacy Coalition Director of Connections

Thank you for the opportunity to look at your book "Praying Deeper through the Psalms for Children". I think it's great how you kept the same weekly Psalms for this book AND "Praying Deeper Through the Psalms for Grandparents & Parents, Too!" This will make using the books together very easy.

I love how your grandsons were able to contribute in a way relevant to their peers and how there are three different age groups from which to choose. I appreciate the analogy of "hide and seek with God" by finding Him in the Bible in your intro. I also enjoyed how your grandsons made application in their own lives, ie: "everyone is mad at me or maybe it's just a few people in my class". I know this will be relatable to all the children who use this as a tool. Thanks for your diligence in passing on useful tools to share our faith with our grandkids!

Sheri Herbruck
Mom, Grandma

I finally got a chance to read the chapters you sent. Great work. I love the structure you used, and the choice of wording is great for the age range you targeted. Very well thought out and presented. Love it!

Elaine McAllister
Mom, Grandma & Author

Dedication -

I dedicate this book to my grandsons, Josiah, Caleb and Shane. It is my heart's desire for you to grow to be teens, then young men and one day old men who love, believe and follow God and His Word. ~ Lynda Freeman

I dedicate this book to all the children who will use it and learn how to talk with God. ~ Caleb Freeman

I dedicate this book to my parents who love me, and to my grandparents and Miss Liz who taught me about Jesus. ~ Shane Freeman

When you think about praying, you probably think about thanking God at meals and saying your prayers before you go to bed. While saying *"Thank You"* to God before you eat and talking with Him before you go to sleep are wonderful times to pray, there is more to praying than just these times.

It may seem hard to pray to Someone Who you are not able to see, but prayer is simply talking with God the way you talk to people you do see; and the great news is God has promised to listen, hear and answer your prayers! Look at these verses in the Old Testament Book of Jeremiah, in chapter 29 verses 9 – 14a . . .

> *"I know the plans I have for you," announces the* LORD. *"I want you to enjoy success. I do not plan to harm you. I will give you hope for the years to come. Then you will call out to me. You will come and pray to me. And I will listen to you. When you look for me with all your heart, you will find me. I will be found by you," announces the* LORD.

God promises in these verses to listen to you when you call out to Him; when you pray. He says when you look for Him with your all, you will find Him! What amazing promises; and God *always* keeps His promises!

The parts of the verses in Jeremiah 29 where they talk about God listening to you and answering your prayers are easy to understand, but what does it mean where it tells you to look for God with your all? Where do you "*look*" for God?

Do you remember playing hide-and-seek? What were your favorite places to hide? Well, while you certainly will not find God hiding under the table, in a closet or behind your sofa, He does promise when you look for Him with your all, you **will** find Him! It is kind of like if you are playing hide-and-seek with God and it is your turn to count while He hides. After you finish counting, you say, "*Ready or not, here I come! Oh where, oh where could You be?!*" God does not stay quiet while He waits for you to find Him; oh not, not at all! He wants you to find Him, so He calls out and says; "*Here I am! I'm in the Bible!*" He gives you His very own words in the Bible. When you read His words, you are able to "find" God!

Yes, the Bible is one of the placeswhere you go to "find" God and the Bible Book of Psalms is a great place to begin! David (the David who fought Goliath and was King of Israel) wrote most of the Book of Psalms. These words tell you how David found God when he went looking for Him . . . and show you how you are able to do the same!

Praying Deeper Through the Psalms for Children will help you look for God with your all. Each week you will find a few verses to read – or have read to you - from Psalms. You will also find key verse(s) along with a Key Word/Thought. Use these to help you think about the point of the passage/prayer all week long.

You might consider writing it on a sticky note and then put it where you will see it all week to remind you of what you are talking with God about and as a reminder to pray.

You will also find some information to help you understand what these verses are saying, help you think about what they mean to you, how you are able to live the verses and how they change your life. Then you will find three "nutshell" prayers.

"What is a 'nutshell' prayer," you ask? Well, a "nutshell" prayer is a prayer which puts what the Bible verses for the week are talking about into just a few sentences; so you are able to understand and pray those verses back to God. A "nutshell" prayer will help you remember what the Bible verses are taking about and help you be able to pray those verses.

The collaborators/illustrators for this project are a pre-teen and children, just like you! Josiah Freeman is in the Sixth Grade and he helped with the first prayer you will find each week. If you read well and are upper-elementary/middle school age, you will probably find this is the prayer you will choose to use when you pray. Caleb Freeman is in Third Grade and he helped with the second prayer. If you enjoy reading or even are new at reading on your own, you will appreciate the shorter prayer as you pray the Bible verses. Shane Freeman is in Kindergarten and he helped his grandma, Lynda Freeman, and his brothers, Josiah and Caleb, think about how to write/draw this prayer each week in a "nutshell," so a non-reader, or brand-new reader, is able to understand and remember the prayer. If you are a non-reader, you will be able to "read" your prayer as it is "written" with simple drawings – and words for your grandparents and/or parents to use to help you. Josiah, Caleb and Shane drew most of these drawings.

Choose whichever prayer "fits" you the best, or use a combination of the prayers to make your own "nutshell" prayer. Feel free to use part of the other prayers and add your own words and/or drawings to make your own prayer.

You will also find space to write your own special requests each week. Do you have a test at school? Are you praying for a friend who is experiencing difficult times? Do you know and love someone who is ill? Do you feel lonely and in need of a good friend? Are you sad about something? Is there something for which you especially want to thank God? Whatever your own prayer requests are, write or draw them in the space provided each week to remind you to talk with God about the things which matter to you. You may be certain, if you care about these things, they are absolutely important to God! Be sure to write or draw when and how God answers your prayers as well!

You might find keeping *Praying Deeper Through the Psalms for Children* near your bed will help you remember to pray each morning when you wake up and each night before you go to sleep. And, of course, as you pray your "nutshell" prayer each day, you may find yourself thinking about and praying your verses throughout your day, too! This is wonderful! Look what the Bible, in the New Testament Book of Ephesians, chapter 6, verse 18 has to say about this . . .

> At all times, pray by the power of the Spirit. Pray all kinds
> of prayers. Be watchful, so you can pray. Always keep on
> praying for all the Lord's people.

God wants you to keep on praying throughout your day! When your "nutshell" prayers from the Book of Psalms come to your mind throughout your day, you will be able to pray them again!

These prayers will help you learn to pray the Scriptures back to God, which will help you learn to find and know God for yourself! Get ready for some exciting times talking to and with God!

And, by the way, if your grandparents and/or parents are using the *Praying Deeper Through the Psalms for Grandparents & Parents, Too!*, you will all be able to pray through Psalms together as the prayers each week in your book, *Praying Deeper Through the Psalms for Children* match what they will be praying in their book!

Information for Grandparents and/or Parents

Praying Deeper Through the Psalms for Children is a tool to help the children you love learn to talk with God. Plan to sit down with your grandchild/child each week to go over the Bible verses for the new week and talk about what they mean. If you are doing this with your grandchild and they live a distance from you, try to connect on-line, over the phone or through email to discover together what they will be praying in the coming week.

If you are using *Praying Deeper Through the Psalms for Grandparents & Parents, Too!*, be sure to remind your grandchildren/children you will be praying with and for them in the coming week as well. Give the ones you love a "hug" each day by praying for them!

Start the week praying together, in person or through tech, and if your grandchild/child is not a reader yet, do the reading for them. Make this a project you do together – just imagine how your and their lives will be blessed by praying through the Psalms together in the coming year! How exciting! Make this a special and fun time – it is a unique opportunity to grow truly close to the children you love, as you help them grow closer to the God Who loves them so much!

Week 1 – Read Psalms 1

Key Verses/Thoughts – Psalm 1:1,2 – Follow
God

So, what is it all about? –

> These verses talk about what it looks like to be wise.
> They describe what a wise person looks like, does and
> what the things look like in which they, "take delight."
> Psalms 1 shows how you are able to make the choice to
> obey God, love His Word and follow Him.

Pay attention to –

- What does God want me to do according to these
  verses?
- What happens when I choose to obey God?
- What do I really like about these verses?
- What do I not like or not understand in these verses?
- How do these verses help me know and find God?
- What will I do today to think about God and His Word?

Pray it in a "nutshell" –

- *Dear God, please help me be wise and choose to follow and obey You; not those who make fun of You or Your Word. Please help me find joy in Your Word and think about it all the time, so I live a fruitful life. Thank You for watching over me! Amen.*

- *Dear God, please help me be wise and want to follow You; not any others. Please help me think about Your words and have joy. Thank You for watching over me! Amen.*

- *Dear God, please help me to be wise and to follow Your words. Please give me Your joy; thank You for watching over me! Amen.* (word "God" for "God, children for "me", owl for "wise", sheep/Shepherd for "follow", Bible for "words", happy child for "joy", children saying "thanks" for "thank You", eyes for "watching over", stick children for "me")

My prayer from Psalms 1 this week –

My prayer list – (Date) - and how God answers –

Week 2 – Read Psalms 3

Key Verse/Thought – Psalms 3:5 – God is with you.

So, what is it all about? –

> These verses talk about how when you feel like people are against you, you are able to know God is for and with you.

Pay attention to –

- What does God want me to do when it feels like others are against me?
- What happens when I choose to talk with and trust God?
- What do I really like about these verses?
- What do I not like or not understand in these verses?
- How do these verses help me know and find God?
- What will I do today to think about God and His Word?

Pray it in a "nutshell" –

- *Dear God, it feels like the world is against me . . . or maybe it is really just a few kids in my class. Please help me as I try to ignore the people who bully me. Help me as I lay in bed, so I am able to sleep without worrying about what will happen tomorrow. Please help me remember You are with me; please help me see and remember how You bless me. Amen.*

- *Dear God, when it feels like others are against me, please help me be kind at school, remember You are with me and see how You bless me! Amen.*

- *Dear God, when it feels like others are against me, please help me remember You are with me! Amen.* (drawing for "God", sad faces for "others against", children for "me", child with a light bulb over head for "please help me remember", word "God" for "You" and children for "me")

My prayer from Psalms 3 this week –

My prayer list – (Date) - and how God answers –

Week 3 – Read Psalms 5

Key Verses/Word – Psalm 5:1,2 - Pray

So, what is it all about? –

> These verses tell you about talking with God, choosing to follow Him, even when others do not and how much God loves you.

Pay attention to –

- What does God want me to do according to these verses?
- What happens when I choose to obey God?
- What do I really like about these verses?
- What do I not like or not understand in these verses?
- How do these verses help me know and find God?
- What will I do today to think about God and His Word?

Pray it in a "nutshell" –

- *Dear God, please listen to me as I pray to You and help me do the right thing, even if nobody else does. Thank You for loving me, Amen.*

- *Dear God please help me remember to talk to You and choose the right thing. Thank You for loving me, Amen.*

- *Dear God thank You for hearing my prayers and for loving me, Amen.* (drawing for "God", children for "thank You", ears/soundlines for "hearing", praying child for "prayers", heart for "love", children for "me")

My prayer from Psalms 5 this week –

My prayer list – (Date) - and how God answers –

Week 4 – Read Psalms 8

Key Verse/Word – Psalms 8:1 – God is
Majestic

So, what is it all about? –

>These verses talk about how God is a great and amazing
>God, how He created you and everything in the universe.

Pay attention to –

- What do these verses tell me about worshiping God?
- How do these verses talk about creation?
- What do I really like about these verses?
- What do I not like or not understand in these verses?
- How do these verses help me know and find God?
- What will I do today to obey these verses?

Pray it in a "nutshell" –

- *Dear God, I want to praise You for being majestic! Thank
  You for everything You created; thank You for making (fill
  in your own words of the things for which you are
  thankful). Thank You for making me; please help me take
  care of Your creation. I praise You, God! Amen.*

- *Dear God You are amazing and majestic! Thank You for making me and the world; thank You for making (fill in your own words of the things for which you are thankful). Please help me know how to take care of it. I love You God! Amen.*

- *Thank You God for making me, creation, (fill in drawings of things for which you are thankful Thank You for being a big God! Amen.* (children for "thank-you", word "God" for "God", children for "me", animals/plants/sun/moon for "creation", draw things for which you are thankful, children for "thank-you" and drawing for "God")

My prayer from Psalms 8 this week –

My prayer list – (Date) - and how God answers –

Week 5 – Read Psalms 20

Key Verses/Word – Psalms 20:6,7 - Answers

So, what is it all about? –

>These verses talk about how God hears and answers prayer, gives help when you need it and He gives you victory. It also talks about praising God for the victory He gives and trusting Him.

Pay attention to –

- What do these verses tell you about prayer?
- What do you learn about your heart?
- What do you really like about these verses?
- What do you not like or not understand in these verses?
- How do these verses help you know and find God?
- What will you do today to obey these verses?

Pray it in a "nutshell" –

- *Dear God, please help me believe You are there for me and answer my prayers; I want to be quick to praise You when You do. Please give me a heart which wants what You want and help me see how You give me success. Please help me stand firm knowing You answer my prayers. Amen.*

- *Dear God please help me want what You want, stand firm knowing You are there for me and answer my prayers. Please help me see all You do for me and be quick to praise You. Amen.*

- *Dear God, thank You for answering my prayers. Please help me see how You are there for me. Amen.* (drawing for "God", children for "thank-you", children for "my", praying child for "prayers", eyes for "see", drawing for "God" and children for "me")

My prayer from Psalms 20 this week –

My prayer list – (Date) - and how God answers –

Week 6 – Read Psalms 21:1-7, 13

Key Verses/Word – Psalms 21:6, 7 – Trust God's Love

So, what is it all about? –

> These verses talk about how God's love for you never ends, He answers your prayers, gives victory, blessings and joy when you trust Him.

Pay attention to –
- What do these verses tell you about how God answers prayer?
- What about trusting God and His love for you?
- What do you really like about these verses?
- What do you not like or not understand in these verses?
- How do these verses help you know and find God?
- What will you do today to obey these verses?

Pray it in a "nutshell" –

- *Dear God, thank You for hearing and answering my prayers. Please give me eyes which see how You answer and the ways You bless me. I trust You and Your great love* for me; thank You for helping me, so I stand firm. I praise You, God! Amen.

- Dear God, thank You for hearing and answering my prayers. Please help me see Your blessings, how You love me and stand firm trusting You. Amen.

- Thank You God for loving me and for hearing my prayers. Please help me love You with all my heart. Amen. (Simple drawings – children for "thank-you", word "God" for God, heart for "love", "children" for "me", sound lines by child's ears and praying child for "hearing" and "prayer", children for "me", heart for "loving", God for "You", heart for "all my heart")

My prayer from Psalms 21:1-7, 13 this week –

My prayer list – (Date) - and how God answers –

Week 7 – Read Psalms 24

Key Verse/Word – Psalm 24:1,2,6 – Seek God

So, what is it all about? –

> These verses talk about how great God is; He created the
> world, everything on it and all of us. In spite of how
> incredible and great He is, God still wants you to know
> and walk with Him. You are able to seek God, so you will
> know Him. When you do, you will find and praise Him.

Pay attention to –

- What do these verses tell me about Who God is and
  what He has done?
- What do I learn about seeking God in these verses?
- What do I really like about these verses?
- What do I not like or not understand in these verses?
- How do these verses help me know and find God?
- What will I do today to obey these verses?

Pray it in a "nutshell" –

- *Dear God, thank You for creating this amazing world in
  which I live; thank You for creating me. Please help me
  have a pure heart, so I am able to know and walk with You*

and see how You bless me. I want to be a person who
seeks You and who praises You. Amen.

- *Dear God, I love this amazing world You made. Thank You*
  for making and blessing me; please help me seek, know
  and walk with You. You are the King of glory and I praise
  You. Amen.

- *Thank You God for making the world, for making me and*
  for the blessings You give me. Please help me seek and
  follow You. Amen. (Simple drawings – children for "thank
  You", word "God" for "God", world for "world",
  children for "me", gift for "blessings", children for
  "me", eyes for "seek", sheep/shepherd for "follow",
  word "God" for "God")

My prayer from Psalms 24 this week –

My prayer list – (Date) - and how God answers –

Week 8 – Read Psalms 25:1-10

Key Verse/Word – Psalm 25:10 – Trust God

So, what is it all about? –

> These verses tell how you may trust God and put your
> hope/confidence in Him. If others bully you, you are able
> to remember you belong to God, He is with you, you are
> able to ask God to show you His ways and know He will
> guide and teach you. God remembers His love and His
> mercy for you instead of your sins.

Pay attention to –

- What do these verses tell me about Who God is and
  what He does for me?
- What do I learn about trusting God in these verses?
- What do I really like about these verses?
- What do I not like or not understand in these verses?
- How do these verses help me know and find God?
- What will I do today to obey these verses?

Pray it in a "nutshell" –

- *Dear God, please help me learn to put my hope and trust in You; especially if others are bullying me or when I'm going through a difficult time. Please make Your ways known to me; teach and guide me, so I know how to follow You. Please help me remember today how You show Your goodness to me. Thank You for Your great mercy and love for me. Amen.*

- *Dear God, when times are hard and others are unkind, please help me know how to trust in You. Please help me see and remember how You show Your love to me; please teach and guide me, so I will follow You. Amen.*

- *Dear God, please help me see and remember how You show Your love to me, so I will follow You. Amen.* (Simple drawings – drawing for "God", children for "me", eyes for "see", light bulb for "remember", word "God" for "You", heart for "love", children for "me" and "I", footprints for "follow", word "God" for "You")

My prayer from Psalms 25:1-10 this week –

My prayer list – (Date) - and how God answers –

Week 9 – Read Psalms 25:11-21

Key Verses/Word – Psalms 25:12,13 –
Follow God

So, what is it all about? –

> These verses talk about how generations change when
> you choose to respect God and let Him teach you which
> way to go. God promises to forgive your sin and when
> you are lonely, sad and need a friend, you are able to
> trust God to be your Friend; He is with you.

Pay attention to –

- What do these verses tell me about Who God is and
  what He does for me?
- What do I learn about trusting God in these verses?
- What do I really like about these verses?
- What do I not like or not understand in these verses?
- How do these verses help me know and find God?
- What will I do today to obey these verses?

Pray it in a "nutshell" –

- *Dear God, thank You for forgiving my sins. Please fill my heart with worship to You and help me follow the path You show to me. Thank You for being my Friend; please help me remember to look to You in the times when I see Your blessings and in the times when my life is sad, lonely and difficult. Amen.*

- *Dear God, thank You for forgiving me. Please help me to worship and follow You every day and to remember You are my Friend always. Amen.*

- *Dear God, thank You for loving and forgiving me. Please help me follow You and remember You are always my Friend. Amen.* (Simple drawings – word "God" for "God", children for "thank You", heart for "love", children for "me", sheep/shepherd for "follow", light bulb for "remember", word "God" for "You", clock for "always", children for "my", children for "friend",)

My prayer from Psalms 25:11-21 this week –

My prayer list – (Date) - and how God answers –

Week 10 – Read Psalms 26

Key Verse/Word – Psalms 26:1 – Follow
God

So, what is it all about? –

> These verses talk about how making the choice to trust
> God, follow Him and depend on His faithfulness is what
> matters. It also points out why it matters to choose wise
> friends who follow God – and for you to be a wise friend
> who does the same.

Pay attention to –

- What do these verses tell me about Who God is and
  what He does for me?
- What do I learn about trusting God in these verses?
- What do I really like about these verses?
- What do I not like or not understand in these verses?
- How do these verses help me know and find God?
- What will I do today to obey these verses?

Pray it in a "nutshell" –

- *Dear God, thank You I am able to know, no matter what I do not have to be afraid, because You are faithful. Please help me choose wise friends who love You and to be a wise friend to others. I want to worship You and what matters the most; knowing You, so I stand secure. Amen.*

- *Dear God, I am so thankful to know, because You are faithful, I am able to trust you, no matter what. Please help me choose and be a wise friend who loves You. I want to know You more than anything or anyone. Amen.*

- *Dear God, thank You for loving me. Please help me love You, and be a wise friend. Thank You for church where I praise You. Amen.* (Simple drawings – word "God" for "God", children for "thank You", heart for "love", children for "me", heart for "love", word "God" in heart for "You", owl for "wise", children for "friends", children for "thank You", church and praise for "church & praise", word "God" for "You")

My prayer from Psalms 26 this week –

My prayer list – (Date) - and how God answers –

Week 11 – Read Psalms 27:1-6

Key Verse/Word – Psalm 27:5 - Safe

So, what is it all about? –

> These verses talk about how God is your Light, Salvation and safe place – you are able to trust Him and stand secure, not feeling afraid no matter what; even if unkind people (or bullies) give you a hard time. Knowing this gives you confidence in place of fear. When knowing God is the One you want and you seek Him the most, you will be able to experience His joy.

Pay attention to –

- What do these verses tell me about Who God is and what He does for me?
- What do I learn about trusting God in these verses?
- What do I really like about these verses?
- What do I not like or not understand in these verses?
- How do these verses help me know and seek God?
- What will I do today to obey these verses?

Pray it in a "nutshell" –

- *Dear God, thank You I am able to know, no matter what – even if bullies give me a hard time, I do not have to be afraid, because You are my source of strength. Please help me trust, find confidence in knowing with You I do not have to be afraid, seek You and know Your joy. Amen.*

- *Dear God, thank You for helping me be confident instead of afraid when I face troubles. Please help me trust You, seek You and know Your joy. Amen.*

- *Dear God, please help me know I am safe with You and shout for joy. Amen.* (Simple drawings – word "God" for "God", children for "me", happy face for "safe", word "God" for "You", happy child for "joy")

My prayer from Psalms 27:1-6 this week –

My prayer list – (Date) - and how God answers –

Week 12 – Read Psalms 27:7-14

Key Verse/Word – Psalms 27:7,8 – Seek God

So, what is it all about? –

> These verses talk about how you are able to call upon
> and seek God and when you do, He will teach you the
> way for you to go. God will never turn you away, so you
> are able to be confident and trust Him as you wait for
> Him to answer your prayers.

Pay attention to –

- What do these verses tell me about Who God is and
  what He does for me?
- What do I learn about trusting God in these verses?
- What do I really like about these verses?
- What do I not like or not understand in these verses?
- How do these verses help me know and find God?
- What will I do today to obey these verses?

Pray it in a "nutshell" –

- *Dear God, please hear me when I call out to You, show me
  Your mercy and answer me. I want to seek You with my*

all; please help me find You, even when it feels like You are far from me; please help me learn to wait for Your answer. Please teach and lead me and give me the confidence to wait for You. Amen.

- *Dear God, please hear and answer my prayers. I want to seek You with my all; please teach and lead me in Your ways and help me learn to wait for how You answer my prayers. Amen.*

- *Dear God, please hear my prayers and help me learn to seek and follow You. Amen.* (Simple drawings – word "God" for "God", ears/sound lines for "hear", children for "my", praying child for "prayers", children for "me", eyes for "seek", sheep/shepherd for "follow", word "God" for "You")

My prayer from Psalms 27:7-14 this week –

My prayer list – (Date) - and how God answers –

Week 13 – Read Psalms 31:1-8

Key Verse/Word – Psalm 31:1 - Refuge

So, what is it all about? –

> These verses talk about when you turn to God for rescue
> from the difficult times in life, you will find He is your
> strong Refuge. You are able to ask God to lead and
> direct you, so you will miss the "traps" in this life which
> will pull you away from Him. Rather than follow what
> people may think is right, you are able to trust in God,
> rejoice in His love, know He is with you.

Pay attention to –

- What do these verses tell me about Who God is and
  what He does for me?
- What do I learn about trusting God in these verses?
- What do I really like about these verses?
- What do I not like or not understand in these verses?
- How do these verses help me know and find God?
- What will I do today to obey these verses?

Pray it in a "nutshell" –

- *Dear God, thank You for being my strong Refuge in both the blessings and challenging times of my life. Please lead me away from the traps in life which will pull me away from You. Please help me trust You, rejoice in Your love, know You are with me and will keep me safe in You. Amen.*

- *Dear God, thank You for being with me in all the times of my life. Please keep me close to You, so I stay far from traps which pull me away from You. Please help me trust You more and more each day so I will love You more and more as well. Amen.*

- *Dear God, thank You for being with me. Please help me stay close and love You always. Amen.* (Simple drawings – word "God" for "God", children for "thank You", children for "me", heart for "love", word "God" for "You", clock for "always")

My prayer from Psalms 31:1-8 this week –

My prayer list – (Date) - and how God answers –

Week 14 – Read Psalms 31:9-24

Key Verse/Word – Psalm 31:14 - Trust

So, what is it all about? –

> These verses tell how when your life is sad, difficult, you
> may experience poor treatment from bullies or just have
> things happening you do not want or like, you are able
> to talk with God, ask Him for help and trust Him to care.
> You are able to know He is with You and will help you.
> God has plans for your life which will bring you blessings
> and joy; you just need to take refuge in Him, call upon
> Him and put your hope in Him.

Pay attention to –

- What do these verses tell me about Who God is and
  what He does for me?
- What do I learn about trusting God in these verses?
- What do I really like about these verses?
- What do I not like or not understand in these verses?
- How do these verses help me know and find God?
- What will I do today to obey these verses?

Pray it in a "nutshell" –

- *Dear God, please help me to trust You to care about and help me when my life is difficult and I experience sad times. I know my life is in Your hands, all of it, and believe You are with me, will help and listen to me. I am so happy to know You have good plans for my life; I will put my hope in You. Amen.*

- *Dear God, I am so thankful to know You care about me at all times and I am able to trust You with my life. Thank You for helping me, listening with I talk to You and for having good plans for my life. Please help me see how You are with me. Amen.*

- *Dear God, thank You for loving and caring about me in the happy and sad times of my life. Thank You I am able to talk with You. Amen.* (Simple drawings – word "God" for "God", children for "thank You", heart for "love", children for "me", happy faces for "happy", sad faces for "sad", clock for "times", children for "my" and "thank You" and "I", talking child for "talk", word "God" for "You")

My prayer from Psalms 31:9-24 this week –

My prayer list – (Date) - and how God answers –

Week 15 – Read Psalms 32

Key Verse/Word – Psalm 32:5 - Confess/Forgive

So, what is it all about? –

> These verses talk about how your sins are a heavy
> burden, but when you choose to confess them to God,
> He forgives and removes them. God wants to teach you
> the right way for you to go with your life; you just need
> to ask Him to do so.

Pay attention to –

- What do these verses tell me about Who God is and
  what He does for me?
- What do I learn about trusting God in these verses?
- What do I really like about these verses?
- What do I not like or not understand in these verses?
- How do these verses help me know and find God?
- What will I do today to obey these verses?

Pray it in a "nutshell" –

- *Dear God, thank You for removing the burden of my sins*
  by forgiving me when I ask for forgiveness. I want to live

how You want me to live; please teach me the right way for me to go throughout my life. Thank You for the joy which comes when I experience Your unfailing love. Amen.

- *Dear God, I am happy to know You will remove the burden of my sins when I ask You for forgiveness. Please teach me the right way for me to go, so I will know the joy which comes with Your love for me which never ends. Amen.*

- *Dear God, thank You for loving and forgiving me. Please help me know how You want me to live. Amen.* (Simple drawings – word "God" for "God", children for "thank You", heart for "love", say the word "forgiving", children for "me", word "God" for "You", children for "me", say the word "live")

My prayer from Psalms 32 this week –

My prayer list – (Date) - and how God answers –

Week 16 – Read Psalms 33:1-11

Key Verse/Word – Psalm 33:1,2 – Praise God

So, what is it all about? –

> These verses talk about praising God, because His Word
> is true and He is faithful in all He does. They go on to tell
> you how you are able to see His love just by looking at
> the world God created and He has plans for you which
> stand firm – through all the generations.

Pay attention to –

- What do these verses tell me about Who God is and
  what He does for me?
- What do I learn about trusting God in these verses?
- What do I really like about these verses?
- What do I not like or not understand in these verses?
- How do these verses help me know and find God?
- What will I do today to obey these verses?

Pray it in a "nutshell" –

- *Dear God, thank You for Your Word. Thank You I am able
  to know it is true and You are faithful to do all You say You*

will do. Thank You for the amazing world You created; thank You for making (fill in some specific things for which you are thankful). The world shows me how You love me; thank You. I want to praiseYou for having plans for me and my life, please help me follow where You lead. Amen.

- *Dear God, thank You for Your Word and for how I am able to know it is true. Thank You for how it tells me about You and Your amazing creation. I want to thank and praise You for (fill in some specific things in this world for which you are thankful). Amen.*

- *Dear God, thank You for making the world and (fill in some specific things in the world for which you are thankful – draw them into your prayer) Thank You for the Bible and for loving me. Amen.* (Simple drawings – word "God" for "God", children for "thank You", world for "world", draw some of your favorite things, children for "thank You", Bible for "Bible", heart for "love", children for "me")

My prayer from Psalms 33:1-11 this week –

My prayer list – (Date) - and how God answers –

Week 17 – Read Psalms 33:12-22

Key Verse/Word – Psalm 33:22 - Hope

So, what is it all about? –

> These verses talk about how people/nations who choose
> to follow God will experience His blessing. People may
> think God is not able to see what they think or do, but
> these verses tell us God does see and He does know.
> When you put your hope in God and His never-ending
> love for you, you will be saved. Trusting God gives you
> hope and will bring you joy.

Pay attention to –

- What do these verses tell me about Who God is and
  what He does for me?
- What do I learn about trusting God in these verses?
- What do I really like about these verses?
- What do I not like or not understand in these verses?
- How do these verses help me know and find God?
- What will I do today to obey these verses?

Pray it in a "nutshell" –

- *Dear God, I want to make the wise choice of choosing to follow You; please help me have open eyes which see the many ways big and small in which You bless me. When I face challenges, please remind me to put my hope and trust in You to save me and not make the mistake of thinking I am able to handle it on my own. When I hope in and trust You, please help me experience Your joy. Amen.*

- *Dear God, please help me make the wise choice to trust and follow You and to put my hope in the never-ending love You have for me. When I do this, please help me see the ways You bless me and experience Your joy. Amen.*

- *Dear God, please help me choose to follow You and to trust the never-ending love You have for me. Amen.* (Simple drawings – word "God" for "God", children for "me", sheep/shepherd for "follow", word "God" for "You", add word "trust", clock for "never-ending", heart for "love", word "God" for "You", children for "me")

My prayer from Psalms 33:12-22 this week –

My prayer list – (Date) - and how God answers –

Week 18 – Read Psalms 34:1-7

Key Verse/Word – Psalm 34:4, 6 - Praise/Prayer

So, what is it all about? –

> These verses talk about praising God at all times – during our blessings and challenges. When we do this, others who are experiencing challenges, will rejoice and praise God with you. When you turn to God and seek Him in prayer, especially when you feel afraid or are experiencing challenges, God promises to hear, answer, deliver and save you.

Pay attention to –

- What do these verses tell me about Who God is and what He does for me?
- What do I learn about trusting God in these verses?
- What do I really like about these verses?
- What do I not like or not understand in these verses?
- How do these verses help me know and find God?
- What will I do today to obey these verses?

Pray it in a "nutshell" –

- *Dear God, thank You for promising to hear, answer, deliver and save me when I take my problems to You in prayer. I want to praise You for being there for me; in the times where I experience Your blessings and in the times when I face challenges. Amen.*

- *Dear God, I want to praise and thank You for being there for me, especially in the hard times of my life and for hearing and answering my prayers. Amen.*

- *Dear God, thank You for helping me and hearing my prayers. Amen.* (Simple drawings – word "God" for "God", children for "thank You", children for "me", ear/sound waves for "hearing", children for "my", praying child for "prayers")

My prayer from Psalms 34:1-7 this week –

My prayer list – (Date) - and how God answers –

Week 19 – Read Psalms 34:8-14

Key Verse/Word – Psalm 34:10 – Seek God

So, what is it all about? –

> These verses talk about how God is Good and all you have to do is to "taste and see"; get to know Him and you will discover how He shows His great mercy and love to you and you are blessed by choosing to hold on to Him. They go on to tell you when you respect and seek God, you will lack nothing you need. If you want to live a long life which pleases God, turn from evil, seek peace, tell the truth and do what is right.

Pay attention to –

- What do these verses tell me about Who God is and what He does for me?
- What do I learn about trusting God in these verses?
- What do I really like about these verses?
- What do I not like or not understand in these verses?
- How do these verses help me know and find God?
- What will I do today to obey these verses?

Pray it in a "nutshell" –

- *Dear God, please help me make the choice today to get to know You better and follow You more closely. When I do, please help me see the ways You show Your goodness, mercy and love to me. Please help me learn how to respect and seek You, so I will make the right and wise choices You want me to do and will hold tightly to You all my life. Amen.*

- *Dear God, I am so thankful to know You will teach me what it means to respect and seek You; I want to get to know You better and live the way You want me to live. Please help me hold tightly to You all my life. Amen.*

- *Dear God, thank You for loving me. Please help me learn to seek and to obey You. Amen.* (Simple drawings – word "God" for "God", children for "thank You", heart for "love", children for "me", eyes for "seek", say "obey", word "God" for "You")

My prayer from Psalms 34:8-14 this week –

My prayer list – (Date) - and how God answers –

Week 20 – Read Psalms 34:15-22

Key Verse/Word – Psalm 34:17, 18 - Prayer

So, what is it all about? –

> These wonderful verses talk about how God's eyes are always on you and His ears are always listening for your prayers. When you pray, God hears and answers. When you are sad, afraid, confused, feel alone, God is close to you to save, encourage and help you. While throughout your life you are likely to have times which are difficult, you are not alone; God promises to save and help you.

Pay attention to –

- What do these verses tell me about Who God is and what He does for me?
- What do I learn about trusting God in these verses?
- What do I really like about these verses?
- What do I not like or not understand in these verses?
- How do these verses help me know and find God?
- What will I do today to obey these verses?

Pray it in a "nutshell" –

- *Dear God, thank You I am able to know, no matter what I face, I do not have to be afraid, because You love me and are with me. Thank You for Your promise to hear when I pray and to answer, save and help me. When I face difficult times, please remind me of these truths. Amen.*

- *Dear God, I am so thankful to know, because You love me, I am able to know You are always with me; You see and hear my prayers and promise to save me. Please help me remember this. Amen.*

- *Dear God, thank You for loving me. Please help me remember when I am sad or afraid, You are with me and hear my prayers. Amen.* (Simple drawings – word "God" for "God", children for "thank You", heart for "love", children for "me", lightbulb "remember", sad child for "sad/afraid", word "God" for "You", children for "me", ear/sound waves for "hear", praying child for "prayers")

My prayer from Psalms 34:15-22 this week –

My prayer list – (Date) - and how God answers –

Week 21 – Read Psalms 46:1-11

Key Verse/Word – Psalm 46:1 - Refuge

So, what is it all about? –

> These verses teach no matter what happens in the world around us, earthquakes, floods, hurricanes, anything, we are always able to know for sure God is our place of safety, He gives us strength and is always there to help us, so we do not have to be afraid. No matter what happens in world governments, God rules over all; He stops wars and it is He who gives peace. You are able to give honor to God, because He is God and He is with us.

Pay attention to –

- What do these verses tell me about Who God is and what He does for me?
- What do I learn about trusting God in these verses?
- What do I really like about these verses?
- What do I not like or not understand in these verses?
- How do these verses help me know and find God?
- What will I do today to obey these verses?

Pray it in a "nutshell" –

- *Dear God, thank You I am able to know, no matter what happens with the weather, anywhere in the world; or even in my own neighborhood or school, I do not have to be afraid, because I know You are with me and You give me strength. I know peace comes from You and You alone are God, so I honor and praise You. Amen.*

- *Dear God, thank You I am able to know, no matter what happens with the weather or anywhere in the world, I do not have to be afraid, because I know You are with me and You give me strength. I honor and praise You, because You are God. Amen.*

- *Dear God, I'm so thankful to know I do not have to be afraid of the weather or anything, because You are God and You are with me. Amen.* (Simple drawings – word "God" for "God", children for "I", children for "thank You", children for "I", afraid child for "afraid", weather for "weather", say anything, word "God" for "You", children for "me")

My prayer from Psalms 46:1-11 this week –

My prayer list – (Date) - and how God answers –

Week 22 – Read Psalms 55:16-23

Key Verse/Word – Psalm 55:22 - Prayer

So, what is it all about? –

> These verses talk about how morning, noon or evening you are able to call out to God and know for sure He will hear and answer you. If others give you a hard time or even bully you, God will answer you. God does not change and He has promised to never leave you, so even if your friend lets you down or hurts you, you are able to trust God, not give up and turn your worries over to Him, because He will keep you going.

Pay attention to –

- What do these verses tell me about Who God is and what He does for me?
- What do I learn about trusting God in these verses?
- What do I really like about these verses?
- What do I not like or not understand in these verses?
- How do these verses help me know and find God?
- What will I do today to obey these verses?

Pray it in a "nutshell" –

- *Dear God, thank You I am able to know, no matter the time of the day or night, no matter what I face, I am able to talk with You and know You will hear and help me. I am happy to know You do not change, so I am able to give my concerns and needs to You. Because I know You will never leave me. Please keep me going today, no matter what I face. Amen.*

- *Dear God, I am so thankful to know, I am able to talk with You day and night and You will never leave me. I trust You. Please take the things which worry me and help me keep going through this day. Amen.*

- *Thank You dear God, for being with me, so I am able to talk with You at all times, day and night. Thank You I am able to tell You about the things which worry me. Amen.* (Simple drawings – children for "thank You", word "God" for "God", children for "me", mouth for "talk", word "God" for "You", clock for "time", sun/moon for "day/night", children for "thank You" and "me", word "God" for "You", sad child for "worry")

My prayer from Psalms 55:16-23 this week –

My prayer list – (Date) - and how God answers –

Week 23 – Read Psalms 56

Key Verse/Word – Psalm 56:3, 4 - Trust

So, what is it all about? –

In this chapter David wrote about how he felt when he was caught by the Philistines and taken to their king. You are able to read about this in 1 Samuel 21. David did not know what was going to happen to him, so he wrote something very powerful in Psalms 56:3, 4 "When I am afraid, I put my trust in you. In God, whose word I praise —in God I trust and am not afraid. What can mere mortals do to me?" David knew Who to trust and he made the choice to do so. You are able to do the same.

Pay attention to –

- What do these verses tell me about Who God is and what He does for me?
- What do I learn about trusting God in these verses?
- What do I really like about these verses?
- What do I not like or not understand in these verses?
- How do these verses help me know and find God?
- What will I do today to obey these verses?

Pray it in a "nutshell" –

- *Dear God, please show Your mercy to me; especially when others are against me, bullying me or just giving me a hard time. Help me remember to trust You when I am afraid. Thank You for noticing when I am sad and life is hard. Please help me remember I am able to know You are for me, because when I call to You for help, You answer. Thank You for being there for me when I need You. Amen.*

- *Dear God, I am so thankful to know You are for me, especially when I feel afraid or others are giving me a hard time, because when I call to You for help, You answer. Please help me always remember to trust You. Amen.*

- *Dear God, thank You for loving me. Please help me remember to talk to You and know You will answer. Amen.* (Simple drawings – word "God" for "God", children for "thank You", heart for "love", children for "me", light bulb for "remember", praying child for "talk to You", word "God" in heart for "You/answer")

My prayer from Psalms 56 this week –

My prayer list – (Date) - and how God answers –

Week 24 – Read Psalms 57

Key Verse/Thought – Psalm 57:9, 11 – Praise God

So, what is it all about? –

> In these verses Dave wrote about when he ran from King
> Saul and hid in a cave. (You are able to read about this in
> 1 Samuel 24.) He told how he was able to talk with God,
> even when experiencing a difficult situation, and
> because God is faithful and loves him, he knew God
> would hear him, so he was able to praise God.

Pay attention to –

- What do these verses tell me about Who God is and
  what He does for me?
- What do I learn about trusting God in these verses?
- What do I really like about these verses?
- What do I not like or not understand in these verses?
- How do these verses help me know and find God?
- What will I do today to obey these verses?

Pray it in a "nutshell" –

- *Dear God, thank You I am able to call out to You when I face difficult times and know You will save me. When others give me a hard time and try to bring me down, please help me remember how much You love me and never stop. I know You are above all and I will always praise You. Amen.*

- *Dear God, thank You for how You always love me and never stop; especially when others give me a hard time. I will always praise You, because You are greater than all else. Amen.*

- *Dear God, thank You for loving me. I know You are amazing and I praise You. Amen.* (Simple drawings – word "God" for "God", children for "thank You", heart for "love", children for "me/I", word "God" for "You", children for "I", worship for "praise", word "God" for "You")

My prayer from Psalms 57 this week –

My prayer list – (Date) - and how God answers –

Week 25 – Read Psalms 61

Key Verse /Word – Psalm 61:5 - Prayer

So, what is it all about? –

These verses talk about how you are able to talk to God about anything and everything from any place where you may be and He will hear and answer.

Pay attention to –

- What do these verses tell me about Who God is and what He does for me?
- What do I learn about trusting God in these verses?
- What do I really like about these verses?
- What do I not like or not understand in these verses?
- How do these verses help me know and find God?
- What will I do today to obey these verses?

Pray it in a "nutshell" –

- *Dear God, thank You I am able to know, no matter what I face, no matter where I am, I am able to talk to You, cry out to You and know for sure You will hear and answer me. Thank You for being my refuge; I thank and praise You for Your love and faithfulness to me. Amen.*

- *Dear God, I am so thankful to know, when things are going well, or when they are not, I am able to talk to You and know You will hear me. Thank You for loving me. Amen.*

- *Dear God, thank You for loving me and for hearing my prayers. Amen.* (Simple drawings – word "God" in heart for "God", happy child for "thank You", heart for "love", children for "me", heart for "love", word "God" in heart for "You", children for "me", ear for "hearing", children for "me", praying child for "prayers")

My prayer from Psalms 61 this week –

My prayer list – (Date) - and how God answers –

Week 26 – Read Psalms 62

Key Verse/Word – Psalm 62:8 - Trust

So, what is it all about? –

> These verses talk about how when life is difficult from
> bullies, scary situations, difficult classes, or any other
> thing, you are able to find rest and hope in God. You are
> able to trust Him and talk to Him any time, because His
> love for you will never fail or end and He sees all you do
> for Him and He will reward you.

Pay attention to –

- What do these verses tell me about Who God is and
  what He does for me?
- What do I learn about trusting God in these verses?
- What do I really like about these verses?
- What do I not like or not understand in these verses?
- How do these verses help me know and find God?
- What will I do today to obey these verses?

Pray it in a "nutshell" –

- *Dear God, thank You I am able to know, no matter how hard my life may be today, I am able to rest in You and know You are my rock and will give me hope. Thank You for loving me with a love which never ends, please help me trust in You and not in anything this world offers. Amen.*

- *Dear God, I am so thankful to know, because You never stop loving me, I am able to trust you, no matter how hard life may look to me today. Please help me choose to trust You alone. Amen.*

- *Dear God, thank You for loving me with a love which never stops. Amen.* (Simple drawings – word "God" for "God", children for "thank You", heart for "love", children for "me", heart for "love", stop sign for "stop")

My prayer from Psalms 62 this week –

My prayer list – (Date) - and how God answers –

Week 27 – Read Psalms 63:1-8

Key Verse/Word – Psalm 63:3 – Praise God

So, what is it all about? –

> These verses talk about seeking and wanting God more than anything, because you know His love is better than anything. When you do, you will think about, praise and talk to God and hold tightly to Him for all of your life.

Pay attention to –

- What do these verses tell me about Who God is and what He does for me?
- What do I learn about trusting God in these verses?
- What do I really like about these verses?
- What do I not like or not understand in these verses?
- How do these verses help me know and find God?
- What will I do today to obey these verses?

Pray it in a "nutshell" –

- *Dear God, thank You I am able to know, You and You alone are God. I want to seek You, praise You, think about You day and night and hold tightly to You all my life, because I know Your love is better than anything this world will offer. Amen.*

- *Dear God, thank You for loving me. I will praise You, learn to know You more and hold tightly to You for all of my life, because I know nothing is better than You. Amen.*

- *Dear God, thank You for loving me. I will praise and love You. Amen.* (Simple drawings – word "God" for "God", children for "thank You", heart for "love", children for "me, I", praise for "praise", heart for "love", word "God" for "You")

My prayer from Psalms 63 this week –

My prayer list – (Date) - and how God answers –

Week 28 – Read Psalms 66:1-9

Key Verse/Word – Psalm 66:4 – Praise God

So, what is it all about? –

> These verses talk about praising God, because He is
> amazing and He does amazing things. It also makes a
> point of reminding people of some of the great things
> God has done – which encourages you to remember
> what He does for you and lets you know God is big and
> powerful enough to keep you from slipping.

Pay attention to –

- What do these verses tell me about Who God is and
  what He does for me?
- What do I learn about trusting God in these verses?
- What do I really like about these verses?
- What do I not like or not understand in these verses?
- How do these verses help me know and find God?
- What will I do today to obey these verses?

Pray it in a "nutshell" –

- *Dear God, I want to shout for joy to You and praise Your great name, because You are awesome and You do amazing things. Thank You for the things You have done for me (list some) and please help me to always have open eyes, so I see the amazing things You do for me. Thank You for holding me tightly to You. Amen.*

- *Dear God, You are so amazing and You do amazing things. Thank you for the amazing things You do for me (list some). Amen.*

- *Dear God, I want to thank and praise You and remember the amazing things You do for me. Amen. (Simple drawings – word "God" for "God", children for "I", children for "thank", praise for "praise", God for "You", light bulb for "remember", draw something "amazing" God did for you, God for "You", children for "me")*

My prayer from Psalms 66 this week –

My prayer list – (Date) - and how God answers –

Week 29 – Read Psalms 66:10-20

Key Verse/Thought – Psalm 66:16 – Tell what God has done

So, what is it all about? –

> These verses talk about how there are times in your life where God allows you to go through difficult, hard times, but He never leaves you and will always show His love by bringing you through when you call out to Him. When this happens, you are able to tell others what God has done for you.

Pay attention to –

- What do these verses tell me about Who God is and what He does for me?
- What do I learn about trusting God in these verses?
- What do I really like about these verses?
- What do I not like or not understand in these verses?
- How do these verses help me know and find God?
- What will I do today to obey these verses?

Pray it in a "nutshell" –

- *Dear God, when I face difficult, challenging times, please help me remember You are with me and You love me. Please remind me to turn to You and talk to You about my problems, big and small and trust You to hear and help me. I will praise You and tell others how You help me. Amen.*

- *Dear God, when I face a hard time, please remind me to talk to You and remember You love me and are with me. Thank You for helping me. Amen.*

- *Dear God, thank You for loving and helping me when sad things happen. I will remember and praise You. Amen.* (Simple drawings – word "God" for "God", children for "thank You", heart for "love", children for "me", sad child "sad things", children for "me", light bulb for "remember", praise for "praise", word "God" for "You")

My prayer from Psalms 66 this week –

My prayer list – (Date) - and how God answers –

Week 30 – Read Psalms 86

Key Verse/Word – Psalm 86:11 - Prayer

So, what is it all about? –

> These verses talk about how only God is God; there is no
> one like Him, so you are able to talk to Him when you are
> facing difficult times, when you need to be forgiven, any
> time and know He will forgive you and teach you the
> right way to go. He loves you, so you are able to know
> God will hear, listen to and answer you, so you are able
> to follow Him with all your heart.

Pay attention to –

- What do these verses tell me about Who God is and
  what He does for me?
- What do I learn about trusting God in these verses?
- What do I really like about these verses?
- What do I not like or not understand in these verses?
- How do these verses help me know and find God?
- What will I do today to obey these verses?

Pray it in a "nutshell" –

- *Dear God, thank You for hearing, listening to and answering my prayers. Thank You for giving me mercy and forgiveness when I turn to You. Thank You for loving me and for teaching me the right way to go. Please help me trust and follow You with all of my heart, because I know only You are God. Amen.*

- *Dear God, I am so thankful to know I am able to talk with You and You will hear, listen to and answer me. Thank You for loving me; please help me follow You with my all. Amen.*

- *Dear God, thank You for loving me. Please help me love and follow You with all my heart. Amen.* (Simple drawings – word "God" for "God", children for "thank You", heart for "love", children for "me", heart for "love", sheep/shepherd for "follow", word "God" for "You", children for "my", heart for "heart")

My prayer from Psalms 86 this week –

My prayer list – (Date) - and how God answers –

Week 31 – Read Psalms 91

Key Verse/Word – Psalm 91:2 - Refuge

So, what is it all about? –

> These verses talk about how you are always able to trust
> God and His faithful love for you no matter what is
> happening – bullies giving you a hard time, difficult class,
> no matter what; you do not have to be afraid. God will
> never leave you; He will always love you and answer your
> prayers.

Pay attention to –

- What do these verses tell me about Who God is and
  what He does for me?
- What do I learn about trusting God in these verses?
- What do I really like about these verses?
- What do I not like or not understand in these verses?
- How do these verses help me know and find God?
- What will I do today to obey these verses?

Pray it in a "nutshell" –

- *Dear God, thank You I am able to know, no matter what I face, I do not have to be afraid, because You are faithful, You love me and I know You will never leave me. Thank You for hearing my prayers and for answering them. Amen.*

- *Dear God, I am so thankful to know, because You do what You say You will do, I am able to trust you, no matter what. Please help me remember You always love me and never leave me. Amen.*

- *Dear God, thank You for loving me for always and for hearing my prayers. Amen.* (Simple drawings – word "God" for "God", children for "thank You", heart for "love", children for "me", clock for "always", ear/sound waves for "hearing", children for "my", praying child for "prayers")

My prayer from Psalms 91 this week –

My prayer list – (Date) - and how God answers –

Week 32 – Read Psalms 92

Key Verse/Word – Psalm 92:1 – Praise God

So, what is it all about? –

> These verses talk about how it is a good thing to praise
> God for His faithful love and all the amazing things He
> does for you. Always watch for how He saves You and
> blesses you, then all of your life – as you grow up and
> even into your old age, you will be able to praise Him;
> and when you do, you will have joy.

Pay attention to –

- What do these verses tell me about Who God is and
  what He does for me?
- What do I learn about trusting God in these verses?
- What do I really like about these verses?
- What do I not like or not understand in these verses?
- How do these verses help me know find God?
- What will I do today to obey these verses?

Pray it in a "nutshell" –

- *Dear God, I want to praise You for Your love for me which never ends and for all the amazing things You do. Please help me have eyes which see all You do today, and throughout all of my life, so I will always praise You. Amen.*

- *I want to praise You today for (fill in this space). Please help me always see what You are doing for me, so I praise You all of my life. Thank You for all the amazing things You do and for loving me for always. Amen.*

- *Dear God, thank You for always loving me. Please help me see (tell something amazing God did) You do for me, so I will praise You. Amen.* (Simple drawings – word "God" for "God", children for "thank You", clock for "always", heart for "loving", children for "me", eyes for "see", draw something amazing God did for you, children for "me" "I", praise for "praise", word "God" for "You")

My prayer from Psalms 92 this week –

My prayer list – (Date) - and how God answers –

Week 33 – Read Psalms 95:1-8a

Key Verse/Word – Psalm 95:3 – God is Great

So, what is it all about? –

> These are more verses about praising God for all He has done; such as creating the world in which we live. They talk about how great God is, how He takes care of you and you need to choose to listen to Him.

Pay attention to –

- What do these verses tell me about Who God is and what He does for me?
- What do I learn about trusting God in these verses?
- What do I really like about these verses?
- What do I not like or not understand in these verses?
- How do these verses help me know and find God?
- What will I do today to obey these verses?

Pray it in a "nutshell" –

- *Dear God, I want to thank and praise You for how great You are and for this amazing world You made. Thank You*

for taking care of me; please help me make the wise
choice to listen to and follow You all of my life. Amen.

- Dear God, there is no one like You. I want to praise You for
making this amazing world and thank You for taking care
of me. Please help me listen to You all of my life. Amen.

- Dear God, thank You for loving me. Please help me listen
to and follow You always. Amen. (Simple drawings –
word "God" for "God", children for "thank You", heart
for "love", children for "me", ear/sound wave for
"listen", feet for "follow", God for "You", clock for
"always")

My prayer from Psalms 95 this week –

My prayer list – (Date) - and how God answers –

Week 34 – Read Psalms 96

Key Verse/Word – Psalm 96:2 – Praise God

So, what is it all about? –

> These verses are a song of praise to God. David praises and thanks God for creation, salvation, for the great things He has done and for how some day He will come to judge the Earth and take us to Heaven.

Pay attention to –

- What do these verses tell me about Who God is and what He does for me?
- What do I learn about trusting God in these verses?
- What do I really like about these verses?
- What do I not like or not understand in these verses?
- How do these verses help me know and find God?
- What will I do today to obey these verses?

Pray it in a "nutshell" –

- *Dear God, I want to praise You for the great and glorious God You are. I want to worship and rejoice in all You have* done, thank You for (fill in the space with something He has done for you). Amen.

- *Dear God, thank You for (fill in the space with something God has done for you). I praise You for how great and glorious You are. Amen.*

- *Dear God, I want to praise You for being the big God You are. Thank You for (draw a picture of something God has done for you). Amen.* (Simple drawings – word "God" for "God", children for "I", praise for "praise", God for "big God", children for "thank You", draw something for which you are thankful)

My prayer from Psalms 96 this week –

My prayer list – (Date) - and how God answers –

Week 35 – Read Psalms 100

Key Verse/Word – Psalm 100:4 – Praise God

So, what is it all about? –

> These verses talk about praising and worshiping God because you know Who He is, He made you and you belong to Him. You are able to thank Him, because He loves you forever, He is good and His faithfulness lasts for all generations – the ones before you, you and the ones who follow you.

Pay attention to –

- What do these verses tell me about Who God is and what He does for me?
- What do I learn about trusting God in these verses?
- What do I really like about these verses?
- What do I not like or not understand in these verses?
- How do these verses help me know God better and find Him?
- What will I do today to obey these verses?

Pray it in a "nutshell" –

- *Dear God, thank You I am able to know You are God; I worship You and praise You. Thank You for making me and for wanting me to belong to You. Thank You for Your never-ending love for me, for Your goodness and faithfulness. Amen.*

- *Dear God, I am so thankful to know, because You are God and You are faithful, You love me forever. I praise You for Your goodness and praise Your name. Amen.*

- *Dear God, thank You for loving me forever. I praise You, because You are God. Amen.* (Simple drawings – word "God" for "God", children for "thank You", heart for "love", children for "me", clock for "forever", children for "I", praise for "praise", God for "You/God")

My prayer from Psalms 100 this week –

My prayer list – (Date) - and how God answers –

Week 36 – Read Psalms 103

Key Verse/Word – Psalm 103:22 – Praise God

So, what is it all about? –

> These verses tell you to praise God and remember all His
> blessings – He forgives your sin, heals you, gives you His
> love, compassion, grace and blessings, leads you,
> chooses to forget your sin and loves you with a never-
> ending, incredible love. You have much for which to
> praise God.

Pay attention to –

- What do these verses tell me about Who God is and
  what He does for me?
- What do I learn about trusting God in these verses?
- What do I really like about these verses?
- What do I not like or not understand in these verses?
- How do these verses help me know find God?
- What will I do today to obey these verses?

Pray it in a "nutshell" –

- *Dear God, I want to praise You for all the ways You show Your love for me. Thank You for the many blessings You have given to me. Thank You for (fill in how God has blessed you). Amen.*

- *Dear God, I want to praise You for all the ways You show Your love for me. Thank You for the many blessings You have given to me. Thank You for (fill in how God has blessed you). Amen.*

- *Dear God, thank You for loving me. I want to praise You for all the ways You have blessed me (draw some of your blessings). Amen.* (Simple drawings – word "God" for "God", children for "thank You", heart for "love", children for "me/I", praise for "praise", God for "You", gifts for "blessed", draw pictures of your blessings, children for "me")

My prayer from Psalms 103 this week –

My prayer list – (Date) - and how God answers –

Week 37 – Read Psalms 107:1-3, 17-32, 41-43

Key Verse/Word – Psalm 107:1 – God is Good &
Loving

So, what is it all about? –

> These verses talk about how thanking God for His love
> for you which never ends. They call upon you to tell
> others the ways God has shown His love to you and then
> tell how He has done this for people through the ages.

Pay attention to –

- What do these verses tell me about Who God is and
  what He does for me?
- What do I learn about trusting God in these verses?
- What do I really like about these verses?
- What do I not like or not understand in these verses?
- How do these verses help me know and find God?
- What will I do today to obey these verses?

Pray it in a "nutshell" –

- *Dear God, thank You for loving me. Please help me
  remember Your love for me will never end. Thank You for*

the ways You show Your love for me (tell some of the ways He does this) – please give me the courage to tell others what You have done for me. Amen.

- *Dear God, thank You for loving me. Please help me remember Your love for me will never end. Thank You for the ways You show Your love for me (tell some of the ways He does this). Amen.*

- *Dear God, thank You for loving me. Thank You for showing Your love for me (draw a couple ways God shows His love for you). Amen.* (Simple drawings – word "God" for "God", children for "thank You", heart for "love", children for "me", children for "thank You", word "God" for "Your", heart for "love", children for "me")

My prayer from Psalms 107 this week –

My prayer list – (Date) - and how God answers –

Week 38 – Read Psalms 108:1-6; 111:1-4, 7-10

Key Verse/Word – Psalm 108:1 – Praise God

So, what is it all about? –

> These verses talk about being determined to praise God with all of your heart for His great, faithful love and because He, and everything He does, is glorious.

Pay attention to –

- What do these verses tell me about Who God is and what He does for me?
- What do I learn about trusting God in these verses?
- What do I really like about these verses?
- What do I not like or not understand in these verses?
- How do these verses help me know and find God?
- What will I do today to obey these verses?

Pray it in a "nutshell" –

- *Dear God, thank You for all the things You do for me, big and small. Thank You for (fill in things He has done for which you are thankful). I want to praise You forever, because You are glorious. Please give me a heart which praises You with my all. Amen.*

- *Dear God, I am so thankful for (fill in with things for which you are thankful) and for knowing You will love me forever. I am praising You with all my heart. Amen.*

- *Dear God, thank You for loving me forever. Please help me see what You do for me, so I will praise You. Amen.* (Simple drawings – word "God" for "God", children for "thank You", heart for "love", children for "me", clock for "forever", children for "me", eyes for "see", God for "You", children for "me", praise for "praise", God for "You") (Draw pictures of what God does for you.)

My prayer from Psalms 108 & 111 this week –

My prayer list – (Date) - and how God answers –

Week 39 – Read Psalms 112:1-9

Key Verse/Word – Psalm 112:1 - Blessed

So, what is it all about? –

> These verses talk about some of the ways God blesses those who respect Himand His Word, are gracious, compassionate, generous and do what is right – their families will be blessed, they will have what they need, stand firm and not be afraid.

Pay attention to –

- What do these verses tell me about Who God is and what He does for me?
- What do I learn about trusting God in these verses?
- What do I really like about these verses?
- What do I not like or not understand in these verses?
- How do these verses help me know and find God?
- What will I do today to obey these verses?

Pray it in a "nutshell" –

- *Dear God, thank You for the many ways You bless me when I choose to follow You. Thank You for (list some of*

His blessings) and thank You for Your promise even when things are difficult, I will be able to see the light – the right way to go. Thank You for the many ways You show Your love for me; please help me see the many ways I am able to show I love You by the ways I show love to others. Amen.

- *Dear God, I am so thankful for Your many blessings; thank You for (list some of the ways God has blessed you). Please help me know how to show I love You by the way I love others. Amen.*

- *Dear God, thank You for (draw some of God's blessings). Please help me show I love You by how I love others. Amen.* (Simple drawings – word "God" for "God", children for "thank You", (draw some of God's blessings), children for "me", heart for "love", word "God" for "You", heart for "love", children for "others")

My prayer from Psalms 112 this week –

My prayer list – (Date) - and how God answers –

Week 40 – Read Psalms 119:1-16

Key Verse/Word – Psalm 119:2 - Blessed

So, what is it all about? –

> These verses talk about how you are blessed when you
> seek and follow God and His Word with all of your heart.
> When you memorize God's Word, think about it and live
> according to what it tells you do to or not to do, you will
> be able to live a pure life which glorifies God.

Pay attention to –

- What do these verses tell me about Who God is and
  what He does for me?
- What do I learn about trusting God in these verses?
- What do I really like about these verses?
- What do I not like or not understand in these verses?
- How do these verses help me know and find God?
- What will I do today to obey these verses?

Pray it in a "nutshell" –

- *Dear God, thank You for giving me Your Word, so I will
  know the right way to live. Please help me want to seek*

You by reading, memorizing and thinking about the things in the Bible. I want to live a life which pleases You. Amen.

- *Dear God, I am so thankful for the Bible, so I will know how to live the way You want me to live. Please help me make time to read it and think about it every day. Amen.*

- *Dear God, thank You for the Bible. Please help me understand it, so I will know how what You want me to do. Amen.* (Simple drawings – word "God" for "God", children for "thank You", Bible for "Bible", children for "me", child/light bulb for "understand", children for "I", God for "You", children for "me")

My prayer from Psalms 119:1-16 this week –

My prayer list – (Date) - and how God answers –

Week 41 – Read Psalms 119:41-56

Key Verse/Word – Psalm 119:43 - Hope

So, what is it all about? –

> These verses talk about how if people tease or bully you
> for believing in God, you are able to trust His Word and
> follow Him, because you know He loves you. When you
> suffer you are able to find comfort in knowing your hope
> in God's Word, so you may choose to follow Him.

Pay attention to –

- What do these verses tell me about Who God is and what He does for me?
- What do I learn about trusting God in these verses?
- What do I really like about these verses?
- What do I not like or not understand in these verses?
- How do these verses help me know and find God?
- What will I do today to obey these verses?

Pray it in a "nutshell" –

- *Dear God, thank You I am able to know, no matter what I face, no matter if others bully or tease me, I am able to find comfort and hope in knowing Your Word is true and You love me. Please help me make the choice each day to hold on to Your Word and follow You. Amen.*

- *Dear God, I am so thankful to know, because You love me, I am able to trust You and Your Word, even if others bully or tease me. Please help me choose to believe Your Word and follow You. Amen.*

- *Dear God, thank You for loving me. Please help me love You and the Bible for always. Amen.* (Simple drawings – word "God" for "God", children for "thank You", heart for "love", children for "me", heart for "love", word "God" for "You", Bible for "Bible", clock for "always")

My prayer from Psalms 119:41-56 this week –

My prayer list – (Date) - and how God answers –

Week 42 – Read Psalms 119:105-120

Key Verse/Word – Psalm 119:105 – Obey God's Word

So, what is it all about? –

These verses talk about how God's Word will help you know the right thing to do throughout your life. You are able to choose to obey the Bible and when you do, you will praise God, experience His joy and grow in your love for His Word.

Pay attention to –

- What do these verses tell me about Who God is and what He does for me?
- What do I learn about trusting God in these verses?
- What do I really like about these verses?
- What do I not like or not understand in these verses?
- How do these verses help me know and find God?
- What will I do today to obey these verses?

Pray it in a "nutshell" –

- *Dear God, I want to thank and praise You for giving me Your Word, so I know the right thing to do. In the blessings and challenging times of my life, please help me hold tightly to Your Word and grow in my love for and trust in it. Amen.*

- *Dear God, I want to thank and praise You for giving me the Bible, so I know the right thing to do. When things go well for me, and when they do not, please help me hold tightly to Your Word and love and trust it more and more. Amen.*

- *Dear God, thank You for the Bible. Please help me always love and trust it always. Amen.* (Simple drawings – word "God" for "God", children for "thank You", Bible for "Bible", children for "me", clock for "always", heart for "love and trust", Bible for "it", clock for "always")

My prayer from Psalms 119:105-120 this week –

My prayer list – (Date) - and how God answers –

Week 43 – Read Psalms 119:124-144

Key Verse/Word – Psalm 119:130 – God's Word

So, what is it all about? –

> In these verses David continues to talk about how he loves God's Word and for help undestanding it, so he will obey. He says the unfolding of God's words gives light and understanding – so it is a wonderful thing to have people who help you understand God's Word.

Pay attention to –

- What do these verses tell me about Who God is and what He does for me?
- What do I learn about trusting God in these verses?
- What do I really like about these verses?
- What do I not like or not understand in these verses?
- How do these verses help me know and find God?
- What will I do today to obey these verses?

Pray it in a "nutshell" –

- *Dear God, thank You for Your Word and for the people who help me understand it. Please help me understand it* more and more, so I will obey it and grow in my love for Your Word. Amen.

- *Dear God, I am so thankful for Your Word. Please give me people to help me understand it, so I will know the right thing to do and will love it more and more. Amen.*

- *Dear God, thank You for the Bible and for the people who help me understand it. Please help me obey and love it always. Amen.* (Simple drawings – word "God" for "God", children for "thank You", Bible for "Bible", grandparents/parents for "people", children for "me", light bulb for "understand", children for "me", heart for "obey/love", Bible for "it", clock for "always")

My prayer from Psalms 119:124-144 this week –

My prayer list – (Date) - and how God answers –

Week 44 – Read Psalms 119:145-152, 162-176

Key Verses/Word – Psalm 119:151, 152, 165 - Prayer

So, what is it all about? –

> These verses talk about talking with God at all times –
> day or night and knowing He is near, hears and answers
> your prayers. God's promises bring you joy and great
> peace; you are able to believe, trust and follow God's
> Word.

Pay attention to –

- What do these verses tell me about Who God is and what He does for me?
- What do I learn about trusting God in these verses?
- What do I really like about these verses?
- What do I not like or not understand in these verses?
- How do these verses help me know and find God?
- What will I do today to obey these verses?

Pray it in a "nutshell" –

- *Dear God, thank You I am able to know, no matter what I face, no matter if it is day or night, I am able to call out to You with all my heart and know You will be near me and answer. Thank You for the peace and joy Your Word gives me; please help me choose to always believe, trust and follow You. Amen.*

- *Dear God, I am so thankful to know you are always near me, no matter what, so I am always able to talk with You. Thank You for Your Word; please help me always obey it. Amen.*

- *Dear God, thank You for loving me. Please help me love Your Bible and follow You. Amen.* (Simple drawings – word "God" for "God", children for "thank You", heart for "love", children for "me", heart for "love", word "God" in heart for "Your", Bible for "Bible", shee/shepherd for "follow", word "God" for "You")

My prayer from **Psalms** 119:145-152, 162-176 this week –

My prayer list – (Date) - and how God answers –

Week 45 – Read Psalms 121, 124, 125, 131

Key Verses/Word – Psalm 125:1, 2 - Trust

So, what is it all about? –

> These verses talk about trusting God, no matter what
> trouble, bullies or sad things come along and knowing
> you are always able to talk with Him, because He is on
> your side and He is with you always.

Pay attention to –

- What do these verses tell me about Who God is and
  what He does for me?
- What do I learn about trusting God in these verses?
- What do I really like about these verses?
- What do I not like or not understand in these verses?
- How do these verses help me know and find God?
- What will I do today to obey these verses?

Pray it in a "nutshell" –

- *Dear God, thank You I am able to know, no matter what I*
  face, You are with me and are watching over me. I am

happy to know You are on my side and are will help me. I trust You and put my hope in You forever. Amen.

- *Dear God, I am so thankful to know You are always with me and are watching over me. Thank You for helping me. I will trust You forever. Amen.*

- *Dear God, thank You for watching over me. I will love You, forever. Amen. (Simple drawings - word "God" for "God", children for "thank You", eyes for "watching over", children for "me", heart for "love", word "God" for "You", clock for "forever")*

My prayer from Psalms 121, 124, 125, 131 this week -

My prayer list – (Date) - and how God answers –

Week 46 – Read Psalms 136:1-9, 23, 26

Key Verse/Word – Psalm 136:1 - Thankful

So, what is it all about? –

> These verses talk about thanking God, because He is good and His love for you never ends. He shows His love in all of creation and in ways He takes care of you. His love never ends – be absolutely sure of this.

Pay attention to –

- What do these verses tell me about Who God is and what He does for me?
- What do I learn about trusting God in these verses?
- What do I really like about these verses?
- What do I not like or not understand in these verses?
- How do these verses help me know and find God?
- What will I do today to obey these verses?

Pray it in a "nutshell" –

- *Dear God, thank You for loving me now and forever and for the many ways You show Your love for me. Thank You when I look at the world around me, I am able to see how much You love me. Thank You when I remember how You (write something God has done for you/your family), I am able to see how much You love me. Amen.*

- *Dear God, I am so thankful to know You love me now and forever and show it in ways I am able to see; such as creation and when You (write something God did for you/your family). Thank You for always loving me. Amen.*

- *Dear God, thank You for loving me forever and for how I am able to see Your love in the world around me and when You (draw a picture of something God did for you/your family).* Amen. (Simple drawings – word "God" for "God", children for "thank You", heart for "love", children for "me", clock for "forever", children for "I", eyes for "see", word God for "Your", heart for "love", world for "world", children for "me", word "God" for "You", your drawing)

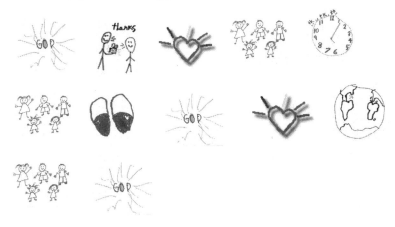

My prayer from Psalms 136:1-9, 23, 26 this week –

My prayer list – (Date) - and how God answers –

Week 47 – Read Psalms 139

Key Verses/Thought – Psalm 139:1, 13-18 –
God's love

So, what is it all about? –

> These verses tell how God knew what He was doing
> when He created you. He knew everything about you
> before you were born and He did not make any mistakes
> in creating you. God thinks about you all the time – He is
> very happy with how He created you – He loves you and
> is always with you.

Pay attention to –

- What do these verses tell me about Who God is and
  what He does for me?
- What do I learn about trusting God in these verses?
- What do I really like about these verses?
- What do I not like or not understand in these verses?
- How do these verses help me know and find God?
- What will I do today to obey these verses?

Pray it in a "nutshell" –

- *Dear God, thank You I am able to know You had a plan when You created me and You love how You made me. It is wonderful to know You love and think about me and are with me any and every place I go. Please help me remember this every day. Amen.*

- *Dear God, I am so thankful to know You had a plan for me before I was born and You are happy with how You made me. Thank You for being with me every place I go. Amen.*

- *Dear God, thank You for loving me and making me with (draw something special about you). Amen.* (Simple drawings – word "God" for "God", children for "thank You", heart for "love", children for "me", draw something special about how God created you – your smile, twinkly eyes, generous heart, kind spirit, bubbly laugh, brave enthusiasm, etc.)

My prayer from Psalms 139 this week –

My prayer list – (Date) - and how God answers –

Week 48 – Read Psalms 141

Key Verses/Word – Psalm 141:1-3 - Prayer

So, what is it all about? –

> These verses are about asking God to keep you safe
> from the "traps" which might draw you towards evil.
> You are able to choose to be a person who keeps their
> eyes on God, talk to God and know He hears you, so you
> live a life which pleases God and keep your eyes on Him.

Pay attention to –

- What do these verses tell me about Who God is and
  what He does for me?
- What do I learn about trusting God in these verses?
- What do I really like about these verses?
- What do I not like or not understand in these verses?
- How do these verses help me know and find God?
- What will I do today to obey these verses?

Pray it in a "nutshell" –

- *Dear God, please do not let me be drawn to things which
  are evil, but instead help me make wise choices, because I*

know when I call out to You, You will hear me and come quickly to help. As I grow up, please help me keep my eyes on You. Amen.

- *Dear God, I am so thankful to know, when I pray to You for help, You hear and help me. Please help me keep my eyes on following You and away from things which take me away from You. Amen.*

- *Dear God, thank You for hearing me when I pray. Please help me keep my eyes on You. Amen.* (Simple drawings – word "God" for "God", children for "thank You", ear for "hearing", children for "me", praying child for "pray", children for "me/my", eyes for "eyes", word "God" for "You")

My prayer from Psalms 141 this week –

My prayer list – (Date) - and how God answers –

Week 49 – Read Psalms 142

Key Verses/Word – Psalm 142:1, 3a - Prayer

So, what is it all about? –

> David wrote these verses when he was hiding in a cave
> from King Saul who wanted to kill him. If you ever feel
> like others are against you, are being bullied, or just feel
> down, these verses are able to encourage you with the
> truth; you are able to call out to God, because He
> watches over you.

Pay attention to –

- What do these verses tell me about Who God is and
  what He does for me?
- What do I learn about trusting God in these verses?
- What do I really like about these verses?
- What do I not like or not understand in these verses?
- How do these verses help me know and find God?
- What will I do today to obey these verses?

Pray it in a "nutshell" –

- *Dear God, thank You I am able to know, no matter what I face, even if I'm being bullied or feel alone, I am not alone; You are watching over me and are with me. Please help me remember to call out to You when I feel down and know You will answer me. Amen.*

- *Dear God, I am so thankful to know, even when I feel sad, bullied or alone, You are with me. I am not alone. Please help me remember to pray when I feel afraid or sad and know You are watching over me. Amen.*

- *Dear God, thank You for hearing me when I am sad or afraid and pray to You. Please help me remember You are with me. Amen.* (Simple drawings – word "God" for "God", children for "thank You", ear/sound waves for "hearing", children for "me", sad child for "sad/afraid", praying child for "pray", word "God" for "You", children for "me", light bulb for "remember", God for "God", children for "me")

My prayer from Psalms 142 this week –

My prayer list – (Date) - and how God answers –

Week 50 – Read Psalms 143

Key Verses/Word – Psalm 143:8, 10 - Prayer

So, what is it all about? –

> These verses talk about praying and how you are able to
> turn to God for help. Even though Satan wants you to be
> defeated, you are able to remember the things God has
> done for you before and trust Him to show you the right
> way to go and to love you forever.

Pay attention to –

- What do these verses tell me about Who God is and
  what He does for me?
- What do I learn about trusting God in these verses?
- What do I really like about these verses?
- What do I not like or not understand in these verses?
- How do these verses help me know and find God?
- What will I do today to obey these verses?

Pray it in a "nutshell" –

- *Dear God, hear my prayer, listen to my cry for mercy;*
  in your faithfulness and righteousness come to my relief.

Please help me remember all You have done for me, show me the right way to go and trust Your love for me forever. Amen.

- *Dear God, I am so thankful to know I am able to trust you to hear my prayer and help me. Please help me remember all you have done for me, tell me the right thing for me to do and trust You to always love me. Amen.*

- *Dear God, thank You for loving me forever. Please help me know how to follow You. Amen.* (Simple drawings – word "God" for "God", children for "thank You", heart for "love", children for "me", clock for "forever", children for "me", sheep/shepherd for "follow", word "God" or "You")

My prayer from Psalms 143 this week –

My prayer list – (Date) - and how God answers –

Week 51 – Read Psalms 144

Key Verse/Word – Psalm 144:2, 14 – God's love

So, what is it all about? –

> These verses tell how any and everything you face in
> your life – the difficult times, times when someone
> bullies you, scary times, sad times – all of them, you are
> able to turn to and trust God to be with you and help
> you. He will not let anything stand between Him and you
> when you need, and ask for, His help.

Pay attention to –

- What do these verses tell me about Who God is and
  what He does for me?
- What do I learn about trusting God in these verses?
- What do I really like about these verses?
- What do I not like or not understand in these verses?
- How do these verses help me know and find God?
- What will I do today to obey these verses?

Pray it in a "nutshell" –

157

- *Dear God, thank You I am able to know, no matter what I face, I am able to turn to You for help and know You will not let anything stand in the way of Your help. I want to praise You for Your love, blessings and power to help me. Amen.*

- *Dear God, I am so thankful to know when I need Your help, You will not let anything stop You from helping me. Thank You for Your love, blessings and power to help me. Amen.*

- *Dear God, thank You for loving me. Please help me remember when I need help, I am able to talk to You and You will help me. Amen.* (Simple drawings – word "God" for "God", children for "thank You", heart for "love", children for "me", light bulb for "remember", children for "I", talking child for "talk", God for "You", children for "me")

My prayer from Psalms Psalm 144 this week –

My prayer list – (Date) - and how God answers –

Week 52 – Read Psalms 145

Key Verse/Word – Psalm 145:3,4,8,9 – Praise God

So, what is it all about? –

> These verses talk about praising God for how great He is,
> the amazing things He does, how He is slow to be angry,
> He is full of love and compassion, is faithful, good, hears
> and answers prayer, watches over you and You are able
> to trust Him. You may tell others how Great God is and
> praise Him forever.

Pay attention to –

- What do these verses tell me about Who God is and
  what He does for me?
- What do I learn about trusting God in these verses?
- What do I really like about these verses?
- What do I not like or not understand in these verses?
- How do these verses help me know and find God?
- What will I do today to obey these verses?

Pray it in a "nutshell" –

- *Dear God, I want to praise You for the many ways You show Your goodness, faithfulness and love to me. Thank You for (fill in things for which you are thankful) Please help me tell others how amazing and good You are. Amen.*

- *Dear God, I want to praise You for how You show Your goodness, faithfulness and love to me. Thank You for (fill in things for which you are thankful). Please help me tell others how You show Your love to me. Amen.*

- *Dear God, thank You for loving me. I want to praise You for (draw pictures of things God has done to show His love for you). Amen. (Simple drawings – word "God" for "God", children for "thank You", heart for "love", children for "me", praise for "praise", word "God" for "You", draw your drawings)*

My prayer from Psalms 145 this week –

My prayer list – (Date) - and how God answers –

About the Creative Team behind this book

 Josiah Freeman enjoys playing his saxaphone, creating music, riding mountain bikes with his family, participating in the annual Mud Run and anything tech.

Caleb Freeman loves dogs, climbing, riding mountain bikes with his family, rocks, participating in the annual Mud Run and using the computer.

 Shane Freeman loves dogs, rocks, learning about space, being able to get very muddy in the annual Mud Run, good jokes and most anything tech.

Lynda Freeman is the very happy grandma to Josiah, Caleb and Shane. She loves spending time with her family and writing. Since she is not very tech minded, she is very thankful her grandsons (and the rest of her family) are! The thing she likes the most about praying the Psalms, is it is something anyone of any age is able to do.

Additional Resources to Hand Down the Faith

Praying Deeper Through the Psalms for Grandparents & Parents, Too! follows the same reading schedule as does *Praying Deeper Through the Psalms for Children.* When parents and/or grandparents use this resource along with the children they love, they are able to pray and learn together. It is available on Amazon.

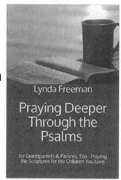

Generations Quest – Cultivate the Faith has 52 complete lessons designed to help grandparents/parents hand down the faith to the children they love. You will find science projects, activities, Bible lessons and information on why we are able to believe God is real and the Bible is true. A must-have tool for your intentional grandparenting/ parenting "tool kit". Also available on Amazon.

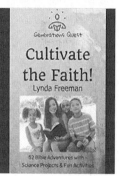

Generations Quest provides you with one year of activities and short daily Bible passages for you, and everyone in your family to read together. As you all discover what the Bible has to say about knowing and walking with God, you will have conversations which matter. Available at https://generationsq.blogspot.com/

Made in the USA
Lexington, KY
17 November 2019

57197052R00105